Family Break-Up

→ how do you cope?

Sarah Medina

www.heinemann.co.uk/library
Visit our website to find out more information about **Heinemann Library** books.

To order:
☎ Phone 44 (0) 1865 888066
🖹 Send a fax to 44 (0) 1865 314091
💻 Visit the Heinemann Bookshop at www.heinemann.co.uk/library to browse our catalogue and order online.

First published in Great Britain by Heinemann Library,
Halley Court, Jordan Hill, Oxford OX2 8EJ, part of Harcourt Education.

Heinemann is a registered trademark of Harcourt Education Ltd.

Editorial: Lucy Thunder and Harriet Milles
Design: David Poole and Kamae Design
Illustrations: Jeff Anderson
Picture Research: Melissa Allison and Kay Altwegg
Production: Camilla Smith

Originated by Ambassador Litho Ltd
Printed and bound in China, by WKT Company Limited

The paper used to print this book comes from sustainable resources.

ISBN 0 431 21035 7
09 08 07 06 05
10 9 8 7 6 5 4 3 2 1

British Library Cataloguing in Publication Data
Medina, Sarah
(Get Wise) – Family Break-Up – how do you cope?
306.8'9

A full catalogue record for this book is available from the British Library.

Acknowledgements
The Publishers would like to thank the following for permission to reproduce photographs:
p. **4** Alamy/Royalty Free; pp. **5, 25, 27** Photofusion/Ulrike Preuss; p. **6** Bubbles/Peter Sylent; p. **7** Bubbles/Lucy Tizzard; pp. **8, 13** Bubbles; p. **10** Alamy/Royalty Free; p. **11** Alamy; p. **12** Education Photos; pp. **14, 24** www.JohnBirdsall.co.uk; pp. **15, 21** Bubbles/Angela Hampton; pp. **16, 20** Getty Images/Photodisc; p. **18** Alamy/Photofusion; pp. **22, 26** Bubbles/Loisjoy Thurstun; p. **23** Photofusion/Joanne O'Brien; p. **28** Corbis/Royalty Free; p. **29** Bubbles/Catchlight

Talk time images pp. **5, 9, 13, 17, 19, 21, 23, 25, 29** Getty Images/Photodisc

Cover photograph reproduced with permission of Alamy/Goodshoot

The Publishers would like to thank Dr Ute Navidi, former Head of Policy at ChildLine, for her assistance in the preparation of this book.

Every effort has been made to contact copyright holders of any material reproduced in this book. Any omissions will be rectified in subsequent printings if notice is given to the Publishers.

Disclaimer
All the Internet addresses (URLs) given in this book were valid at the time of going to press. However, due to the dynamic nature of the Internet, some addresses may have changed, or sites may have changed or ceased to exist since publication. While the author and Publishers regret any inconvenience this may cause readers, no responsibility for any such changes can be accepted by either the author or the Publishers.

Important note: If your family is breaking up, or has broken up, and you feel that you can't cope, go straight to the **Getting help** box on page 31. There are phone numbers to call for help and support.

Contents

Words appearing in bold, **like this**, are explained in the Glossary.

Family matters

What is a family – and why are families important?

What is a family? Do you think of a family as a married mother and father with two children? If so, you are not alone! This is the picture that many people have of a typical family.

Which family are you?

Nowadays, though, family life is likely to be much more varied. For example, some parents do not get married. Many people live in a **step-family**. Then there are some children who live with **carers** who are not their parents. These could be grandparents, aunts and uncles, **adoptive parents** or **foster parents**.

Families – however they appear – are important to us all. We learn many things from our families – from how to talk to how to deal with the world as adults. Most of us receive lots of love and support from our families, too.

Adverts on TV often ➲ show families looking like this – with two married parents and two kids. But, these days, families can look very different!

Breaking up

Sadly, families sometimes break up. Parents who are married may get **divorced**. **Cohabiting** parents may decide not to live with each other any more. This is very hard for everyone at first, and it often brings about many changes.

🎧 Families in the 21st century come in all shapes and sizes.

If you are going through family break-up, this book will help you to understand more about what is happening. It will also give you suggestions about how to cope and where to get help. Don't worry – although things may feel really hard now, they will get better, bit by bit.

Talk time

What is your family like?

Tanvi: I live in a big family – with my mum and dad, three brothers and sisters, and my grandma and grandad.

Scott: I'm an only child, and I live with my mum, because my parents got **divorced**. I see my dad during school holidays.

Rick: My mum and dad got divorced, too, and now I live with my dad and my step-mum, and my two step-brothers.

Lei-Lei: My parents aren't married, but they have lived together for fifteen years – since before my older sister was born.

Newsflash

According to a BBC *Newsround* survey, there are now lots of different kinds of families. For example, there are families like the cartoon Simpsons with three children, two birth parents – plus dippy dog and crazy cat. Or there are 'jigsaw' families, like pop star Madonna and her husband Guy Ritchie, who have Madonna's daughter from another relationship living with them.

Splitting up

Why do parents break up?

Breaking up is always painful – and most people take a long time to decide to split up. When people fall in love, they usually want to be together forever. They never imagine that, one day, they may feel that they cannot live with each other any more. Sadly, sometimes things do not work out.

What happens?

People split up for all sorts of reasons. Sometimes, people just drift apart. They may find that they do not enjoy each other's company any more. Perhaps they argue a lot, which is really stressful. Adults, like young people, often change as they get older. This may mean that they may start to see life differently. They may want to do different things or to be with someone else.

When people decide to split up, it is almost always because one or both of them are very unhappy and want things to change. Even though change is often very hard, they usually believe that splitting up will be better for everyone in the long term.

Top thoughts

'It's been very painful, and it's been emotional and very hard work, but I think I've come out of [my divorce] feeling stronger and clearer about the future and myself.'

Jude Law, actor

If you are ➲ very unhappy together, living with someone else can feel impossible.

Kim's story

Kim's parents used to argue all the time – about everything! The family never had any fun together. Kim and her brother, Dan, didn't dare to do anything wrong, in case it made things worse.

'In the end, Mum and Dad decided to split up. They told us that they still loved us, but that they had stopped loving each other. Dad moved out, and Dan and I stayed with Mum. At first, it was horrible – we missed Dad loads. But we did see him every weekend, and we phoned him every day. To be honest, things got much more chilled at home after Dad left. Mum and Dad are both much happier now – and we all have more fun than we used to.'

◗ Parents may try hard to pretend everything is OK, especially in front of the children. But, sometimes, **separating** becomes their only choice.

THINK IT THROUGH

Should parents stay together for the sake of their children?

Yes. Breaking up hurts children a lot, and parents shouldn't hurt their own children.

No. When parents are unhappy, their children are miserable, too.

What do YOU think?

It's not your fault

Can you ever be to blame for your parents splitting up?

It is really hard if your parents do not get on with each other. Hearing them argue, or just feeling the tension in the air if they are not speaking to each other, is very stressful. It can be scary, too. It can feel as if things are completely out of control when two grown-ups shout or cry, or slam doors or storm out – or simply act as if the other person is not there.

Who is to blame?

If you are in this situation, you may feel that everything is your fault. If you have a brother or sister, try asking them how they feel. You will see that they probably blame themselves, too. You may think that your parents would not have any problems if you behaved perfectly. It is normal to feel this way – but it is not true that you are to blame for your parents' problems.

When parents argue, their problems are always with each other – and only with each other. If your parents **separate** or **divorce**, it is because they were not able to work out their differences. This can be very sad but, in the end, it may be the best solution for everyone.

↺ Remember – children are not responsible for the things their parents say and do to each other.

What sorts of things might children blame themselves for?

It is normal to want to 'glue' your parents back together again – but sometimes this just will not work for them.

Rick: Children might think that their parents will get upset and angry if they fall out with their brothers or sisters and be more likely to split up...

Tanvi: Yeah, and they might feel that they should always do as they are told.

Scott: Like tidying their room or helping around the house.

Lei-Lei: But their parents must have much bigger problems than these if they split up.

THINK IT THROUGH

Is it wrong for parents to argue in front of their children?

Yes. It can be frightening for young people to hear adults arguing – especially their parents.

No. It doesn't hurt children to hear their parents arguing. Everyone argues sometimes.

What do YOU think?

That spinning feeling

How can you cope with the feelings you get if your parents split up?

If your parents tell you that they are going to **separate**, you may feel such a huge rush of different feelings that you feel as if you are spinning. Sometimes it can all seem too much to cope with. Remember, this is a very normal reaction to a very difficult situation. You won't always feel this way – and you are not alone.

It's OK

If your parents break up, you may feel sad, scared, angry, confused, guilty or alone. You may even feel relieved or happy, if things have been hard. Whatever you feel is OK. The best way to deal with your feelings is by talking them over with someone you can trust.

↩ Seeing your parents break up can be really sad. Crying is a healthy way to let out some of your feelings.

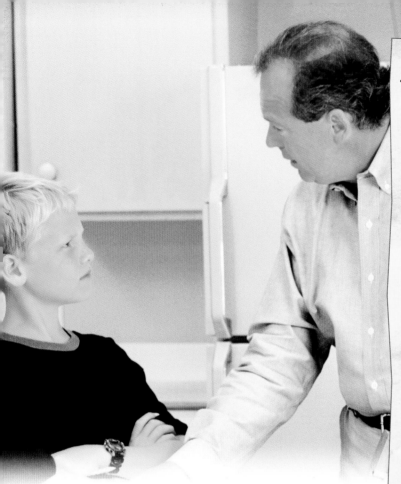

Delroy's story

When Delroy's parents told him they were going to get divorced, he felt really worried about his future.

'I just couldn't stop thinking about it. Mum and Dad agreed with me that I would stay at home with Mum, so I wouldn't have to change schools or anything. But I worried about how we would manage without Dad. Would we have enough money to live on? Would I still be able to go to football and judo and stuff? It was horrible.

'I felt upset and angry for ages but, after a few months, I started to get used to the way things were. Life went on – it was just different. Now, I think that Mum and Dad splitting up has made me stronger. In the future, I'll be more able to cope with other difficult things that might happen.'

It is normal and OK to feel angry with your parents for separating. These feelings will settle down after a time.

THINK IT THROUGH

Is it possible to get over the shock of your parents separating?

Yes. Things always get better after a while. People can get used to a new situation quite quickly.

No. People are affected by their parents' separation forever.

What do YOU think?

Top thoughts

'[My parents' divorce] is something that took me a very long time to come to terms with.'

Angelina Jolie, actress

Who can you talk to when you need to?

If your parents **separate**, it is a difficult time for everyone. You may find it hard to talk to your parents about how you feel. Perhaps you think they have enough to cope with already. And yet, at times like this, it is very important to talk about your feelings, so that they do not get out of control. You may also have lots of questions that need proper answers. If you can, try talking to your parents first of all. You may be surprised at how much they understand and can support you.

A listening ear

If it is hard to talk to your parents, you could try talking to someone else you trust – such as a brother or sister, an aunt or uncle, or a grandparent. Most people will be glad to help you if they can. You could also talk to a friend, or to a teacher or **counsellor** at school.

In many countries there are **organizations** you can contact for help about family break-up (see page 31 for more information). You can phone them for free, and a specially trained person will support you in any way they can. Remember – don't ever be afraid to ask for help.

Writing things ➲ down can help you work out your feelings.

Talk time

What kind of things might children want to ask their parents?

Scott: Who I'm going to live with – Mum or Dad – and where? I'd want to know who was going to look after me.

Rick: Yeah, and whether I'd have to move house or change schools.

Lei-Lei: I'd want to know where I was going to keep all my stuff.

Tanvi: Yeah, and who was going to look after my pet rabbit.

Newsflash

....

A Welsh school has brought in a full-time 'agony aunt' to help pupils to deal with problems such as family break-up. '**Divorce** and parents separating is a really big issue at the moment,' says counsellor Margaret Yeoman. 'I listen and we talk about it, and I try to help them see the whole picture and help them make the right choice if they can.'

....

THINK IT THROUGH

Will it help to talk to your parents?

Yes. Your parents love you and will do all they can to help you.

No. If your parents are separating, they do not have time to talk to you.

What do YOU think?

🎧 Talking about your problems to a friend stops them from building up inside.

What happens when parents separate or divorce?

When parents **divorce** or **separate**, it can be a difficult time for the whole family. As well as coping with all sorts of different feelings, there are a lot of practical things that have to be done. For example, one parent will have to move out of the family home and find a new place to live. Parents may need to talk to **lawyers** or **mediators** to help them agree about new arrangements.

By order of the court

When people live together without getting married, they do not have to do anything special when they separate. They just agree that they will not live together anymore.

When people are married, it is different. Although married people can also decide to stop living together, the marriage itself can only be ended by **law**. To get divorced, married people need a special **court order** made by a **judge**. This can often take several months to sort out.

Sometimes, parents see 🎧 a special mediator to help them decide what they want to happen after separation.

Fact Flash

Some court orders say which parent the children will live with, and how often the children will get to see their other parent.

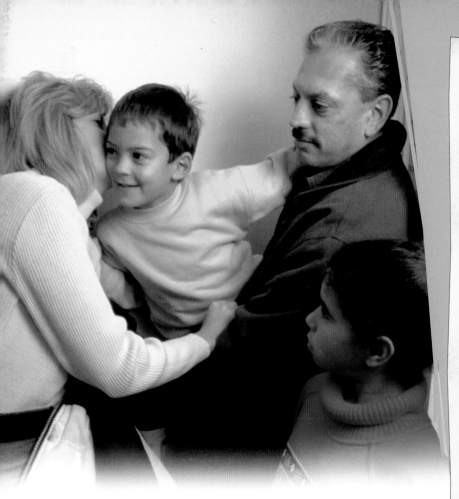
🎧 Your parents may choose to live apart – but you will normally still get to spend plenty of time with each of them.

Marian's story

Things changed a lot for Marian and her brother after their parents divorced. Marian chose to live with her mum, but her brother stayed with their dad.

'Mum and I moved to a small village about an hour away. I had to start a new school, which was pretty scary.

'I do miss my dad and my brother, but we see each other a lot, and we're always phoning and texting. I was sad about leaving my old school friends behind, but I'm still in touch with them – and I've made lots of new friends in my new school, which is really cool.

'I can't say I'm happy that Mum and Dad split up, but I've got used to it now, and I do like my new life.'

THINK IT THROUGH

Should children have a say about arrangements after their parents split up?

Yes. Any decisions affect them, so children should be able to say what they would like to happen.

No. Children do not understand the whole picture, and so they may not know what the best decision is.

What do YOU think?

How should you expect to be treated if your parents are breaking up?

It usually takes people a long time to decide to break up – because it is a very hard choice to make. If your parents are **separating** or getting **divorced**, you may find that they are very stressed. Like you, they have a lot of feelings to deal with. They might seem quite **distracted**, and they may not make as much time for you as they normally do. You might feel quite alone, but remember that your parents both love you and want what is best for you.

Stuck in the middle?

Sometimes, parents do get it wrong. Some parents even try to use their children as 'piggies in the middle' to get things that they want from the other parent. This is very upsetting – and is also unfair. Children deserve to be treated well and with **respect**, no matter how their parents feel or how angry they are with each other.

That 'piggy in the middle' feeling…

The right way

It might be quite hard but, if your parents are doing or saying things that upset you, try to tell them that you don't like it. Then tell them what you *do* want. If your parents feel upset and tired because they are breaking up, they may sometimes have to make an extra-special effort to do things right for you.

Talk time

How might parents behave towards each other after splitting up?

Lei-Lei: They might be really angry, and not talk to each other.

Tanvi: Some parents get their children to give messages to each other instead.

Scott: Yeah – and that's really horrible for the children! They might feel they have to take sides.

Rick: It's much better when parents can just talk to one another and **respect** each other.

THINK IT THROUGH

Should parents who have separated ask their children to give messages to each other?

Yes. Why not? It might be the easiest way for them to communicate.

No. It can make kids really feel uncomfortable. Parents should talk to each other directly.

What do YOU think?

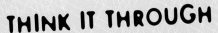

🔊 You are a special person with important views. You should expect your parents to listen to you carefully.

Things that change

What sorts of things change after family break-up – and how can you deal with them?

Top thoughts

'We all have big changes in our lives that are more or less a second chance.'

Harrison Ford, actor

When parents break up, families change. This can feel worrying at first, but remember that change does not always have to be a bad thing. Some people think that change is like a new chance – to do and learn new things, and to meet new people. Without change, we can easily get bored!

Past change

Do you remember your first day at school? You may have felt worried about meeting new people, and about what to do. Now that you have been going to school for a few years, you know who everyone is, and what you have to do each day. You may have quite a lot of fun at school, too! You can see, just from this one example, how you have coped with change in the past. **Divorce** or **separation** is a huge change but, with help and support, you will be able to cope with it, too.

Starting a new ➲ school or club might make you nervous at first. But after a while it will feel as if you have always been there.

Future change

Not everything will change when your parents separate, but some things will. One of your parents will leave the family home, and this means that they will not be around every day. From now on, you will visit them and have **contact** with them in a different way. Depending on your situation, you may need to move house or change schools, and this will mean making new friends, too.

Talk time

What day-to-day things might change if your parents separate?

Scott: If one of your parents moves out, then some of the things you used to do together might change.

Rick: Yes, like when you have meals and when you go to bed.

Lei-Lei: You might have to help more around the house.

Tanvi: Especially if the parent you live with starts a new job.

Some people refuse to change!

THINK IT THROUGH

Is change scary?

Yes. Change is really frightening, because you don't know if new things will work out.

No. Every day is different – and so every day there are changes! Change is normal.

What do YOU think?

Can anything stay the same if parents split up?

Even if your parents **separate** or **divorce**, many of the things you are used to will stay the same. First, and most important of all, your parents will continue to love you and to look after you. The parent who moves out of the family home should still stay involved with decisions that affect you. You will still be able to see them, write to them, and chat to them by phone, text or email.

Friends united

Remember that family and friends will still be there for you, no matter what happens. If you can, spend lots of time with them – and do fun things together. This will give you a break and will help you to feel better. If you have to move to a new place, you can still visit or keep in touch with the people who are important to you.

Top thoughts

'Love seeks only one thing: the good of the one loved.'

Thomas Merton, writer (1915–1968)

Not everything changes ➔ when parents break up. You can still laugh and enjoy fun times with friends and family.

Talk time

What kinds of things might stay the same if your parents separate?

Tanvi: Well, you still have to get up and go to school!

Lei-Lei: Yeah, and do homework and stuff.

Rick: And you still get to hang out with family and friends.

Scott: Yes, and do things you enjoy, like sports or other hobbies.

Chen's story

'When my parents split up a couple of years ago, I was gutted – I thought everything would change. Some big things did, like Mum moving out, and that was really hard. Not everything changed, though.

'There are always things you do regularly, and you do stick to them – at least, most of them. School goes on, for one! I still play football every week, and Mum still comes to watch. Even though I spend every other weekend at Mum's house, I still get time to hang out with my mates.'

🎧 After separating, some parents still get together to do important things, such as parent-teacher meetings at school.

THINK IT THROUGH

Should parents who separate try to keep things exactly the same for their children?

Yes. Parents should make sure that their children do everything they used to, so they don't feel too upset.

No. It's impossible to keep things the same after family break-up, and everyone has to get used to this.

What do YOU think?

How can you stop worrying about your parents?

If parents **separate** or **divorce**, the whole family is likely to feel very mixed up for a while. Parents often worry about how the break-up is going to affect their children. Children can worry just as much about their parents – for example, they worry that they will be lonely or that they will not be able to cope.

Getting used to change

If you can, try not to worry about your parents. Remember that they are adults, and they know what they are doing. It may be difficult for a time but – like you – they will get used to the changes in their lives, and they will be fine.

Staying close

After family break-up, most children live most of the time with one parent, and have regular **contact** with the other. Sometimes, it may not be possible to see the other parent as much as you would like, especially if they move away to live in a different area. However, there are lots of ways you can stay close to each other.

You can choose many ➲ ways to stay in touch with a parent you are not living with, such as chatting online.

Talk time

What can you do to stay close to a parent you do not live with?

Rick: The main thing is to talk on the phone as much as you can.

Lei-Lei: You can also send emails or texts.

Tanvi: Or letters! They're all much cheaper than phoning.

Scott: Chatting online's a good way to stay close, too.

🎧 Remember that your parents have friends and other family members who can help them.

Kate's story

When her Mum moved abroad, Kate worried about losing touch with her.

'I've been living with Dad since Mum left two years ago. Mum met someone else and moved to Spain. I was really worried I'd lose touch with Mum completely. She's busy so she can't come over here much – and it's expensive for Dad to send me there.

'Anyway, Dad bought a computer, and now I email Mum every week. She always emails back, even if it's just a few lines. It really helps. I'd still like to see Mum more than I do, but at least I don't feel quite so far away from her now.'

THINK IT THROUGH

Is it up to you to make your parents feel OK?

Yes. If your parents feel bad, you have to help them to feel better.

No. You are not responsible for your parents' happiness.

What do YOU think?

A new friend

What happens when a parent meets someone new?

Fact Flash

In the UK, about 300,000 children have parents who have been married to another person before.

Parents only usually reach the decision to **separate** or **divorce** when there is no other choice left. You may really want your parents to get back together again. However, this hardly ever happens. In fact, after a time, one (or both) of your parents may even start to see someone new. They may go on to live with or marry this new person, and they may even decide to have a baby.

Little by little

It will probably feel very strange at first to see your mum or dad with another **partner**. You will need time to get to know each other, little by little. As you do this, try to be nice to your mum or dad's new friend. Don't just decide you won't like them from day one! Remember, they are not there to take your place in your parent's heart – or to 'replace' your other parent. And they probably feel just as nervous about getting to know you as you do about them!

You may find that your parent's new partner – and maybe a new brother or sister – become a very special part of your life.

24

Some parents marry their new partners. This can be a fresh, new start for everyone.

Talk time

How can you get to know a parent's new partner better?

Scott: By talking to them when they're around, and not ignoring them!

Lei-Lei: Yes, if you spend time with them, that will help you get to know each other.

Rick: Even just watching TV together is a good start.

Tanvi: It's not just up to you, though. You've both got to make an effort.

Ruben's story

Ruben was worried that he might not get on with his Dad's new partner, until he found out that she liked the same sort of stuff he liked.

'I knew my Dad had been seeing someone after my parents got divorced, but it was ages before I met her. Then, one day, we all went swimming.

It was really weird at first. Steph wasn't anything like Mum. I didn't know if I'd like her – but she's really into sport, like me. We even support the same football team! I'm sure it's going to be OK now.'

THINK IT THROUGH

Is it good for a parent to have a new partner?

Yes. Everyone deserves to be loved and be happy.

No. It is hard for children to get used to someone new being around.

What do YOU think?

Is it possible to live happily in a step-family?

All over the world, millions of children live with a **step-parent** and with a **step-brother** or **step-sister**. **Step-families** come together when somebody lives with or gets married to a person who has children already.

Home or away

In some cases, children live with their step-family when their parent's new **partner** moves into the family home. In other cases, children visit their step-family when their other parent starts living with someone new. Some children share their time equally between one step-family and another.

Everyone has different ➲ habits – some of them not as nice as others! But everyone can learn to live together, especially if they talk about things together.

New rules for all!

Some children settle down quickly and feel very happy with their step-family. Others can find it hard to adapt to step-family life. When two families join together, there may be lots of changes that everyone has to get used to. There may be new rules – about mealtimes, for example. You may feel that you are expected to do things you don't want to, such as sharing your bedroom or your things with someone new. Some children worry that their parent will no longer be able to spend time with them.

You may find that it is good fun having more people in the house to do things with!

Talk, talk, talk!

It is very important to talk to someone you trust about how you feel. You won't spoil anything by telling your mum or dad that you are worried or unhappy. Families are there to help each other – and that includes you! If you really can't speak to your family, talk to someone else you trust, such as a teacher or a **counsellor** at a young people's helpline (see page 31). Remember – you are not alone!

TOP TIPS

It can be hard getting to know new people. Try out these top tips to help!

◎ First of all, give it time! Don't feel that you have to be best friends straightaway.

◎ Spend time with them. Tell them about yourself – and ask them lots of questions, too.

◎ If you can, suggest doing something fun together.

THINK IT THROUGH

Can step-families get along together well?

Yes. It just takes a bit of time and effort to get to know each other.

No. It is hard for people from different families to get along.

What do YOU think?

Can life really be happy again after family break-up?

Hearing that your parents are going to **separate** is usually a huge shock. You can feel as if you have been turned upside down and shaken about. There are so many different feelings to deal with. This is a difficult time for everyone in the family, and you all need a lot of help and support. Although you will have to cope with many changes, you can do it – and you can still be happy about many things.

Better for them ...

Before they split up, your parents probably tried really hard to make things work. But then they realized that the best thing to do – even though it was difficult – was to separate or **divorce**. Now, they can build new lives and find happiness in other ways.

... and for you

Family life may have changed – but this is still your family, and it is still special. It may sound strange, but you could get to spend more quality time with each of your parents after one of them has moved out of the family home. You might get to know them better than ever, and do fun things together that you didn't have a chance to do before. If one or both of your parents starts to live with someone new, you could find that you have a whole new family to enjoy.

🎧 You may find that you get to spend much more time with each of your parents after they have separated. Because they are happier, you may have happier times, too.

Talk time

How might life get better after family break-up?

Tanvi: The atmosphere at home might be loads better, because your parents are not fighting so much.

Lei-Lei: You might have been worried or scared before, and now you know that things are going to be OK.

Scott: Yeah, especially once you've got used to different changes.

Rick: And lots of good stuff can happen – like getting a new **step-family**, which can be really cool.

🎧 Coming through a difficult situation will make you a stronger person. This means you will be able to understand and help more when friends have problems, too.

THINK IT THROUGH

Do you think that coping with difficulty makes you a stronger person?

Yes. If you have coped with one difficult situation, you know that you can cope with anything!

No. Every situation is different. You might be good at coping with one situation, but not with another.

What do YOU think?

Glossary

adoptive parent adult who becomes the legal carer of a child, even though the child was not born to them

carer someone who looks after children but who is not their parent

cohabiting when two adults live together

contact get in touch with, or spend time with a parent

counsellor person who is specially trained to help people to work out their problems

court order when a judge says that something has to happen by law

distracted when a person is not paying attention because they are thinking of something else

divorce when a marriage is ended by law

foster parent adult who looks after a child whose own parent cannot look after them for a time

judge person in charge of a court of law

law rules made by the government of a country that must be obeyed

lawyer person who works with things to do with the law

mediator specially trained person who works with families who are separating, to help them to work out the best way to do things

organization large group of people, all working together to achieve the same aims

partner word used for 'boyfriend' or 'girlfriend' for adults

respect treat someone as if their feelings and opinions are important

separate stop living together

step-family a parent's new wife, husband or partner, and his or her children and relatives

step-brother son of a step-parent

step-parent new wife, husband or partner of a child's parent

step-sister daughter of a step-parent

Check it out

Check out these books and websites to find out more about divorce and separation, and to get help and advice.

Books
Fiction

It's Not the End of the World, Judy Blume (Macmillan, 1998)

Divorce Express, Paula Danziger (Macmillan, 1987)

The Suitcase Kid, Jacqueline Wilson (Random House, 1997)

Websites

ChildLine (UK): www.childline.org.uk

Kidscape (UK): www.kidscape.org.uk

Kids Help Line (Australia): www.kidshelp.com.au

National Childline Helpline (NCH) (UK): www.itsnotyourfault.org

Getting help

If you feel very worried or upset about your parents splitting up, you may need to talk to someone urgently. You can speak to an adult you trust, or you can phone a helpline for support.

- In the UK, you can phone ChildLine free on 0800 1111 (open 24 hours a day). Please remember that calls to 0800 numbers are free, and do not show up on phone bills. You can also write to them at Childline, Freepost NATN1111, London E1 6BR.
- In Australia, you can phone Kids Help Line on 1800 55 1800 (open 24 hours a day).

Index

Titles in the *Get Wise* series include:

Hardback　　0 431 21032 2

Hardback　　0 431 21003 9

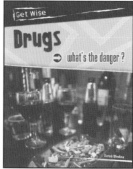

Hardback　　0 431 21004 7

Hardback　　0 431 21002 0

Hardback　　0 431 21035 7

Hardback　　0 431 21033 0

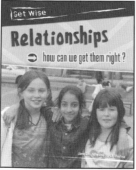

Hardback　　0 431 21036 5

Hardback　　0 431 21000 4

Hardback　　0 431 21001 2

Hardback　　0 431 21034 9

Find out about other titles from Heinemann Library on our website
www.heinemann.co.uk/library